ALL THE NATIONS OF AFRICA
By Mike Donovan

The nations of Africa are listed from smallest to largest in population, from Seychelles to Nigeria.

SEYCHELLES
Population 98,929

The Seychelles Islands, in the Somali Sea, has been an independent nation since 1976. The capital is Victoria. Wavel Ramkalawen is the president.

175 Square Miles of Seychelles

The President of the Republic of Seychelles, Wavel Ramkalawen

SAO TOME AND PRINCIPE
Capital: Sao Tome

The population of Sao Tome and Principe is 259,159. It is an island nation in the Gulf of Guinea. Evaristo Carvalho is the president.

Sao Tome and Principe has been independent of Portugal since 1975.

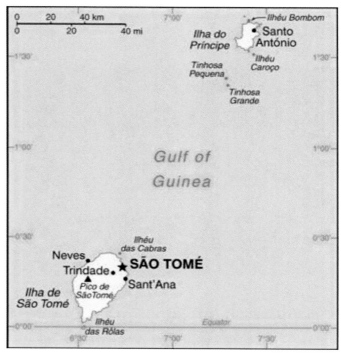

S.T. & P

President Carvalho of Sao Tome & Principe

MALDIVES

The Maldives are 120 square miles of land off the southwest coast of India. 540,544 live there.

The capital is Male. The President of Maldives is Ibrahim Mohamed Solih. Maldives became independent of the United Kingdom in 1965.

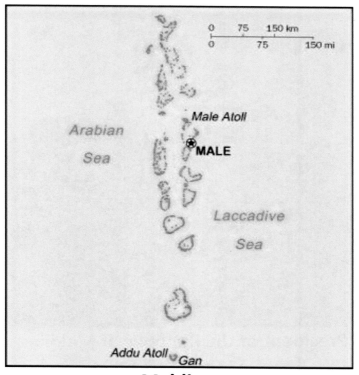

Maldives

**The President of the Republic of Maldives,
Ibrahim Mohamed Soli**

CAPE VERDE

The nation of Cape Verde is in the Atlantic Ocean, 300 miles west of the tip of West Africa.
The Capital is Praia.

Cape Verde has been independent since 1975.

Cape Verde Islands - 1,557 Square Miles

President of Cabo Verde - Jorge Carlos Fonseca

Cape Verde box; Use this map to check your progress memorizing the other nations of Africa

COMOROS

The population of the Comoros Islands is 869,601. The President of the Union of Comoros is Azali Assoumani. It has been French-free since 1975.

The Comoros are east of Africa and north of Mozambique. Moroni is the capital.

719 sq. mi

DJIBOUTI

Shake your Djibouti. This country is about to break the million-person barrier. There are 988,00 people there.

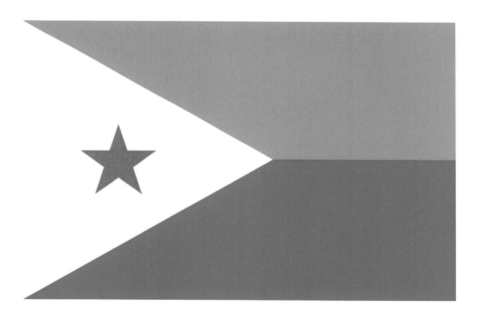

Djibouti has been independent since June 27, 1977. It is 9,000 square miles, and the President is Ismail Oscar Guelleh.

Ismail O. Guelleh, President of Djibouti

ESWATINI

1,160,164 people live in the landlocked Kingdom of Eswatini. It is surrounded by South Africa and Mozambique.

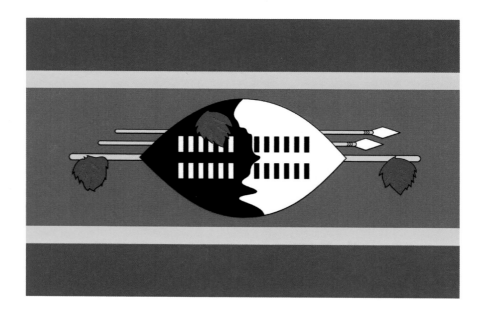

Eswatini was formerly known as Swaziland, but people confused it so often with Switzerland, that it decided (2018) to change its name.

There are two capitals. The legislative capital is Lobama. The executive capital is Mbabane. It is 6,704 square miles large.

The acting Prime Minister of Eswatini is Themba N. Masuku.

Eswatini

Sadly, the Kingdom of Eswatini lost its Prime Minster, Ambrose Dlamini, to Covid 19 on December 13 of 2020. Mr. Dlamini was 52.

The Late Mr. Dlamini

MAURITIUS
Population: 1,271,768

The President of Mauritius is Prithuirasing Roopun. It is 790 square miles small and has been independent since 1968.

President Roopun of Mauritius

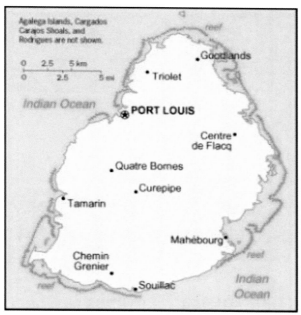

Mauritius

EQUATORIAL GUINEA
Pop.: 1,402,985

The capital of Equatorial Guinea is Malabo, but a new capital is almost completed. The new capital will be Cuidad de la Paz. Equatorial Guinea is 10,830 square miles. The president is Teodoro Manque.

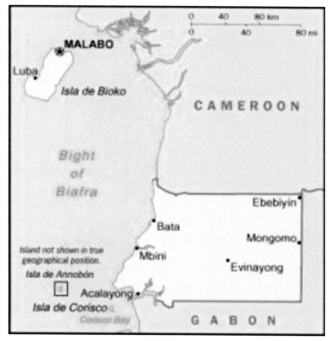

E.G.

Teodoro Manque, President of Equatorial Guinea

GUINEA BISSAU

Guinea Bissau, bordered by Senegal and Guinea, is 13,948 square miles, and home to 1,968,001 people.

Guinea Bissau has been independent since 1974. The president of GB is Umaro S. Embalo.

Guinea Bissau

President Umaro Embaro of Guinea Bissau

LESOTHO

Lesotho is surrounded by South Africa, the largest (11,720 sq. mi.) country in the world that exists within another country (San Marino and the Holy See are the other two.)

The capital of Lesotho is Maseru. The Prime Minister is Moeketsi Majoro.

Moeketsi Majuro, Prime Minister of Lesotho

Lesotho

GABON
Population: 2,225,734

The capital of Gabon is Libreville. Gabon is 103,347 square miles and the current leader is President Ali Bongo Ondimba.

Independent since 1960, Gabon has had only three presidents.

Gabon

Ali Bongo Adima, President of Gabon

BOTSWANA

There are 2,351,627 people in Botswana. The capital and largest city is Gabarone. Botswana shares a border with South Africa, Namibia and Zimbabwe.

The president of Botswana is Mokgweetsi Masisi. It is a large country of 224,610 square miles.

Botswana

Mokgweetsi Masisi, President of Botswana

GAMBIA
Population: 2,416,668
Capital: Banjul

'The Gambia' is the formal name of Gambia. It is almost surrounded by Senegal. The President of the Gambia is Adama Barrow. The Gambia became independent of Britain in 1965.

Adama Barrow, President of Gambia

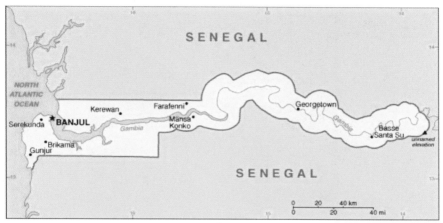

Gambia

NAMIBIA

There are 2,540,905 Namibians. The capital city is Windhoek.

The Beautiful Flag of Namibia

Namibia became independent of South Africa in 1990. The head of state is President Hage Geingob. The land of Namibia is 318,772 square miles.

Namibia

President of Namibia, Hane Geingob

ERITREA

The President of Eritrea is Isaias Afwerki.

The population of Eritrea is 3,546,421. The capital is Asmara. Eritrea became independent of Ethiopia in 1993. It is 45,400 square miles.

President Afwerki of Eritrea

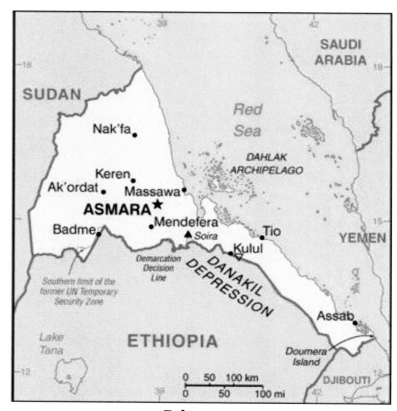

Eritrea

MAURITANIA

The West African nation of Mauritania is home to 4,649,000 people. Nouakchott is the capital.

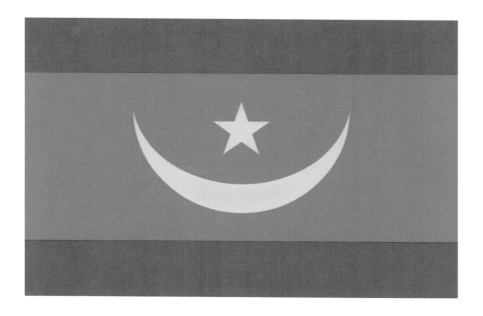

Mauritania, 400,000 square miles big, became independent of France in 1960.

The president of this Islamic republic is Mohamed Ould Ghazuani.

Mauritania

CENTRAL AFRICAN REPUBLIC

The population of this aptly named landlocked country is 4,829,767 people.

The capital of the CAR is Bangui.

The President of the Central African Republic is Faustin-Archange Touadera. The CAR broke free of France in 1958 and became certified independent in August 1960.

The CAR is 240,535 square miles

C.A.R. President Faustin-Archange Touadera

LIBERIA

The capital of Liberia is Monrovia, named, of course, after President James Monroe. Liberia has a population of 5,057,681 people.

George Weah is the President of Liberia. The country became in independent in 1847. Liberia is 43,000 square miles.

Liberia

President George Weah of Liberia

REPUBLIC OF THE CONGO

The Republic of the Congo has been independent since 1960. The capital city is Brazzaville. It is not to be confused with the larger neighbor, the Democratic Republic of the Congo. Population: 5,518,642.

The President of the Republic of the Congo is Denis Sassou Nguesso. It is 88% Christian.

Republic of the Congo: 132,000 sq. mi.

Congo President Denis Sasou Nguesso

LIBYA

The Prime Minister of Libya is Abdul Hamid Dbeibeh. Tripoli is the capital. Libya has been independent of Italy since 1947.

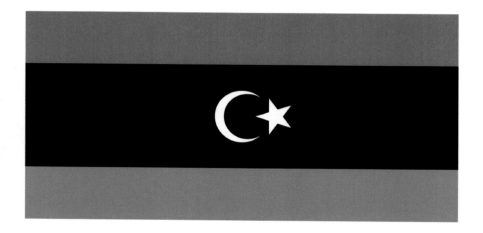

The population of Libya is 6,871,292.

Libya: 679,292 square miles

Libyan Prime Minister Abdul Hamid Dbeibeh

SIERRA LEONE
Pop: 7,976,983
Cap: Freetown

Sierra Leone gained its independence from Great Britain in 1961. The President of Sierra Leone is Julius Maada Bio.

Sierra Leone - 27,700 square miles

Julius Maada Bio, President of Sierra Leone

TOGO

Togo was once (when under German rule) called 'Togoland.' The capital of this West African nation is Lome.

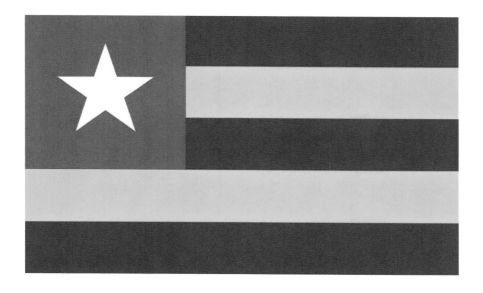

The population of Togo is 8,278,983. The President of Togo is Faure Gnassingbe. Togo has been independent since 1960.

Faure Gnassingbe, President of Togo Since 2005

Togo is 21,925 square miles

SOUTH SUDAN
Population: 11,193,725
Capital: Juba

South Sudan is one of the youngest countries in the world. It became independent of the Sudan in July of 2011. The President of South Sudan is Salva Kir Mayar Dit.

Salva Kir Maya Dit, President of South Sudan

South Sudan: 239,285 sq. mi.

TUNISIA

The capital of Tunisia is Tunis. The population is 11,818,619. Tunisia has been independent of France since 1956.

The President of the Republic of Tunisia is Kais Saied.

63,170 Tunisian sq. mi.

President Kais Saied of Tunisia

BURUNDI

Burundi has two capitals. Bujumbura is the one that I grew up knowing, but Gitega is now the political capital. Bujumbura is the economic capital.

The population of Burundi is 11,890,784. Burundi has been independent of Belgium since 1962. The President of Burundi is Evariste Ndayishimiye.

Burundi: 10,747 sq. mi.

Evariste Ndayishimiye of Burundi

BENIN

Ex-Dahomey, Benin became independent of France in 1960. The capital is Porto Novo. Benin is home to 12,123,200 people.

The current President of Benin is Patrice Talon.

44,310 sq. mi.

The President of Benin, Patrice Talo

RWANDA

The President of Rwanda, a nation of 12,952,218 people, is Paul Kagami. The capital of Rwanda is Kigali.

Rwanda has been independent of Belgium since 1962. A tragic civil war gripped the nation in the 1990s. It has been called the Rwandan Genocide.

Rwanda: 10,169 sq. mi.

President Paul Kagame of Rwanda

GUINEA

The President of Guinea is a real alpha-male. His name is Alpha Conde. 13,132,795 people live in Guinea.

Guinea has been independent of France since 1958. The capital is Conakry.

Guinea is 94,926 square miles

President Alpha Conde of Guinea

ZIMBABWE
Population: 14,862,934
Capital: Harare

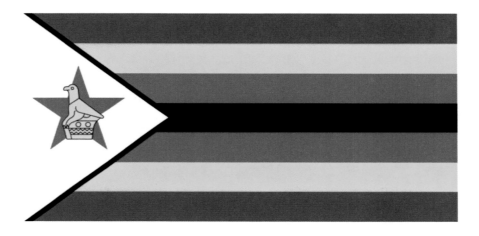

The top banana in Zimbabwe today is President Emmerson Mnanagagwa. The first president of Zimbabwe, elected in 1980, was Caanan Banana.

The nation declared its independence of Britain in 1965, and it was 15 years (as 'Rhodesia') of political limbo before true freedom arrived in 1980.

Zimbabwe: 152,872 sq. mi.

President Emmerson Mnanagagwa

SOMALIA

Somalia has been independent of Italy and Britain since 1960. The President of Somalia is Mohamed Abdullahi Mohamed, of the Toya Party.

The capital of Somalia is Mogadishu. The population is 15,893,222.

246,201 square miles

President Mohamed Abdulahi Mohamed

CHAD

The President of Chad is Idriss Deby. Chad has been independent since 1960. It declared its independence in 1958 and France accepted it in 1960.

16,425,864 people live in Chad. The capital is N'Djamena.

Chad

Idris Deby of Chad

SENEGAL

The President of Senegal is Macky Sall.

The population of Senegal is 16,743,927.

The capital of Senegal is Dakar.

Senegal became independent of France in 1960.

President Mackey Sall of Senegal

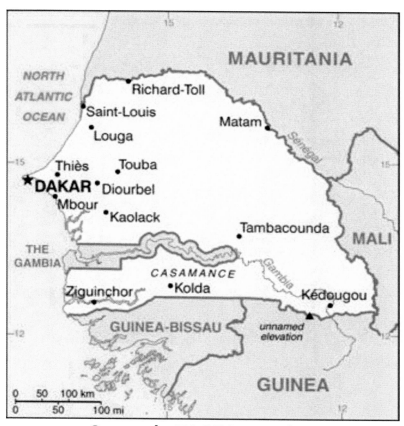

Senegal - 71,951 sq. mi.

ZAMBIA

The President of Zambia is Edgar Lungu. Zambia has been independent since 1964.

Zambia is home to 18,383,955 people. The capital is Lusaka.

President Edgar Lungu of Zambia

290,587 Zambian sq. mi.

MALAWI

The Capital of Malawi is Lilongwe. The President of Malawi is Lazarus Chakwera of the Malawi Congress Party. Chakwera is also the Malawi Minister of Defense.

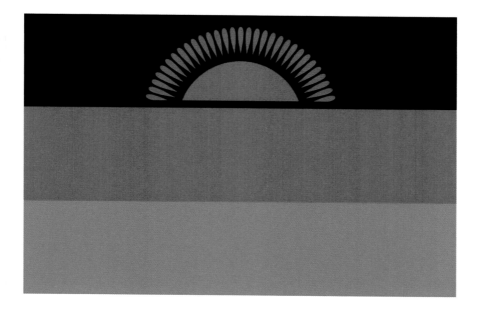

Malawi has been independent of France since 1964. The population is 19,129,952. It is 47,747 square miles.

President Lazarus Chakwera

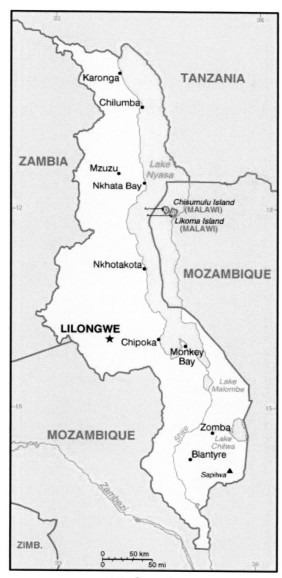

Malawi

MALI

The capital of Mali is Bamako. 20,250,833 people live there. The (interim) President is Bah Ndaw.

Mali has been independent of France since 1960.

Bah Ndaw in Bamako

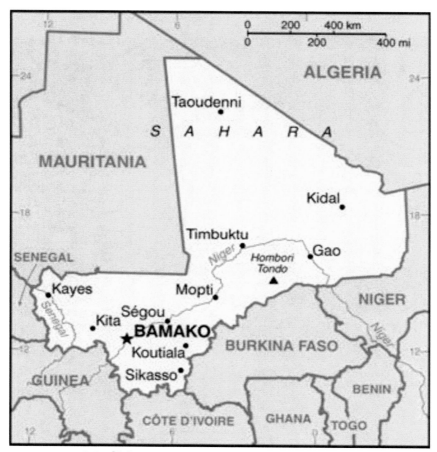

Mali is 478,841 square miles

BURKINA FASO

Burkina Faso used to be called 'Upper Volta.' It became 'BK' in 1984. The capital is Ouagadougou.

The President of Burkina Faso is Roch Marc Christian Kabore. It is 105,900 square miles. The West African state has been independent of France since 1960.

The President of Burkia Faso:
Roch Marc Christiain Kabore

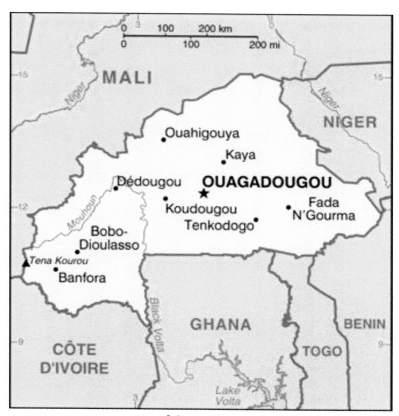

Burkina Faso

NIGER

The capital of Niger is Niamey. The population is 24,206,644. It is 489,000 square miles.

The President is Mahamadou Issofou. Niger has been France-free since 1960.

President Issofou of Niger

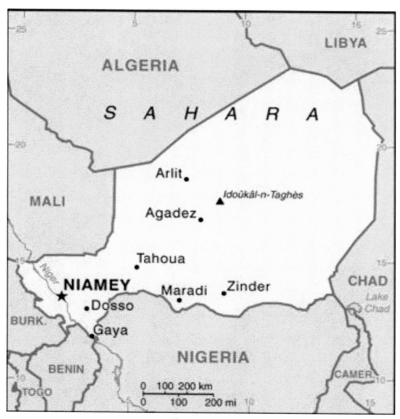

Niger

COTE D'IVORIE
The population of Cote d'Ivorie is **26,378,274.**

The nation I once learned in school as 'The Ivory Coast' is now called Cote d'Ivorie. It has two capitals. Abidjan is the 'de facto' capital and Yamoussoukro is the 'de jure.' Abidjan is the nation's largest city.

The country has been independent since 1960.

President Alessane Ouattare

Cote d'Ivorie - 124,504 sq. mi.

CAMEROON
Capital: Yaoundé
Pop.: 26,545,863

The President of Cameroon is Paul Biya. Cameroon has been independent since 1961.

Cameroon Prime Minister Biya

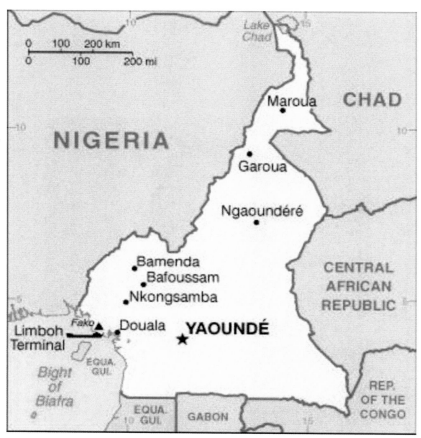

Cameroon is 183,569 sq. mi.

MADAGASGAR

27,691,018 people live in Madagascar, the great island nation off the coast of southeast Africa. The President of Madagascar is Andry Rajoelina. It has been independent since 1960.

(A patch of white on the left of the flag)
The capital of Madagascar is Antananarivo.

President A. Rajoelina of Madagascar

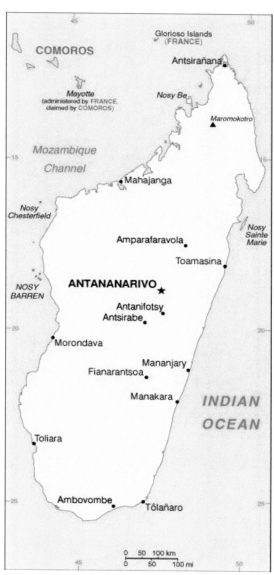

226,658 sq.mi.

GHANA
Capital: Accra
Sq. Mi.: 92,497
Pop.: 31,072,940

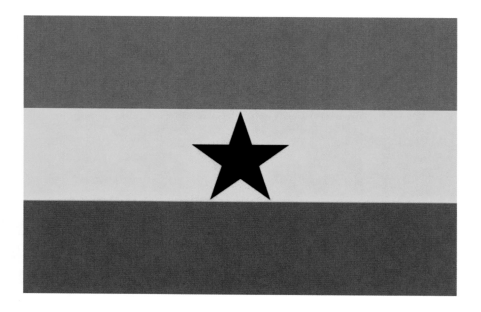

Ghana has been independent since 1960.

The President of Ghana: Nana Akufo-Addo.

Ghana (92,497 sq. mi.)

MOZAMBIQUE

Mozambique has been independent of Portugal since 1975. The capital is Maputo.

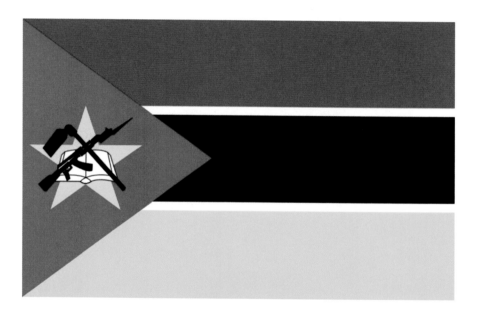

The population of Mozambique is 31,255,435. President Nyusi is the nation's leader.

President of Mozambique: Philipe Nyusi.

309,500 sq. mi. Moz.

ANGOLA

32,866,272 people live in Angola. The capital is Luanda.

Angola became independent (of Portugal) in 1975. The President of Angola is Joao Lourenco.

Angola - 481,440 sq. mi.

President Lourenco of Angola (since 2017)

MOROCCO

The Prime Minister of Morocco is Saadeddine Othmani. Rabat is the capital. Casablanca is the largest city in Morocco.

36,910,560 people live in this North African nation. Morocco has been independent since 1956.

Morocco is 274,460 square miles.

Prime Minister Othmani

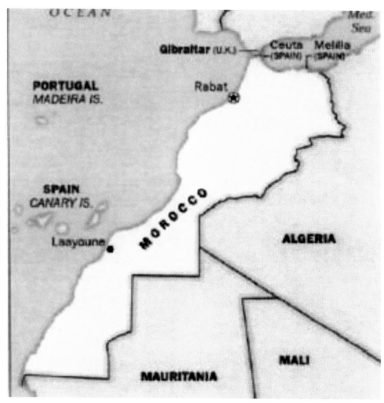

274,460 Square Morocco Miles

SUDAN
Population: 43,849,260
Khartoum is the capital and largest city in Sudan

Sudan became free of foreign (G.B.) rule in 1956 to secession in 2011. The Prime Minister is Abdallah Hamdok.

Sudan Prime Minister Hamdok

Sudan is 728,215 square miles

ALGERIA

43,851,044 people live in the North African country of Algeria.

The capital is Algiers.

Algiers fought a tough civil war with France and emerged victorious and independent in 1962. The President of Algeria is Abdelmadjid Tebboune.

President Tebboune

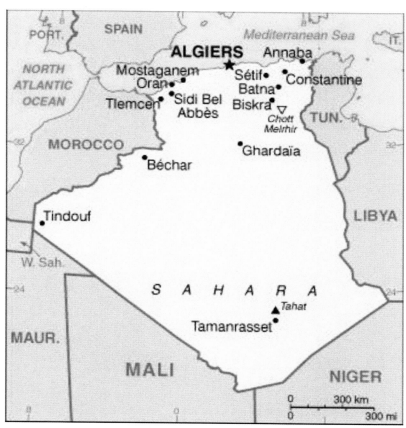

#10 in size - 919,515 sq. mi.

UGANDA

The capital of Uganda is Kampala, not far from Entebbe. The President of Uganda is Yoweri Musivini. It has been independent since 1962, when it broke from U.K. rule. 45,741,007 people live in Uganda.

Uganada President Musivini - since 1986

Uganda - 93,065 square miles

KENYA

The capital of Kenya is Nairobi. The population is 53,771,236. The President of Kenya is Uhuru Kenyatta.

Kenya disunited from the United Kingdom in 1963. The UK accepted Kenyan independence in 1964.

Uhru Kenyatta

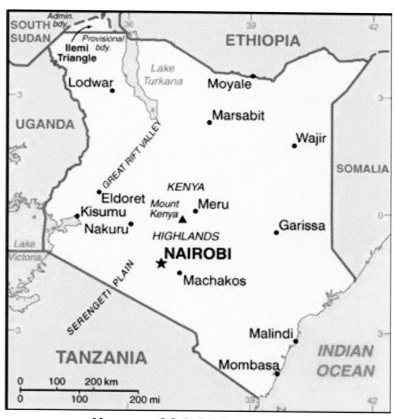

Kenya -224,081 sq. mi.

SOUTH AFRICA

The one-time British colony has been independent since 1911, and a new democracy since 1994. There are 59,308,690 people who call South Africa home. The capital is Pretoria, although Cape Town and Bloemfontin share the chores. It is the only nation that claims three national capitals.

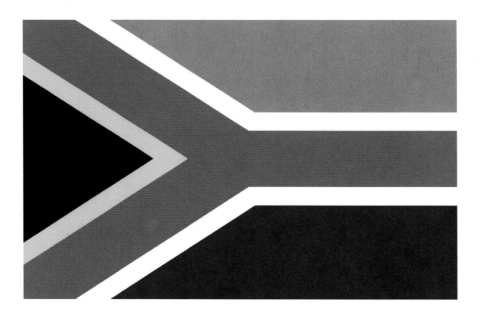

President Cyril Ramaphosa of South Africa

South Africa - 471,445 square miles

TANZANIA
Capital: Dodoma/Dar Es Salaam
Population: 59,734,218

The largest city is Dar es Salaam. Tanzania became independent as Tanganyika in 1961, from Great Britain.

The President of Tanzania, John Magufuli.

365,756 sq. mi

DEMOCRATIC REPUBLIC OF THE CONGO

The DRC became independent of Belgium in 1960. It changed its name to Zaire in 1971 & to the DRC in 1997.

The capital of the Democratic Republic of the Congo is Kinshasa. The population is 89,561,403. A second source has the population at 103,000,000, but I am staying with the uniform stats of 'World-o-Meter.'

President of the DRC, Felix Tshisekidi

At 905,567 sq. mi., DRC is the 11th largest country in the world.

EGYPT
  Since 3150 B.C.!
  Capital: Cairo
  Population: 102,334,404

The President of Egypt is Abdel Fatah el-Sis.

The President of Egypt, Abdel Fattah el-Sisi

Egypt: 390,121 sq. miles

ETHIOPIA
Capital: Addis Ababa
People: 114,963,588

The President of Ethiopia is Sahle-Work Zewde. Ethiopia has been independent since 1941.

President of Ethiopia Sahle-Work Dewde

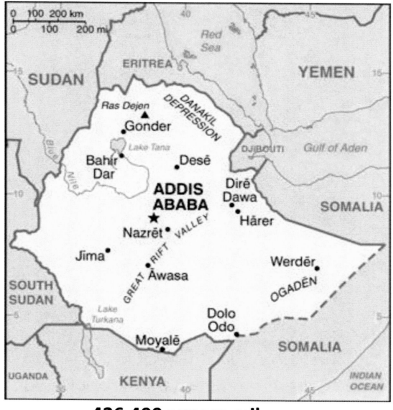

426,400 square miles

NIGERIA
Capital: Abuja.
Population: 206,139,589

There were 50 million people living in Nigeria in 1971. It has quadrupled in size since then. The President of Nigeria is Muhammadu Buhari.

Nigeria is a large oil producer and a member of OPEC. It has been independent of the U.K. since 1960. Lagos is the largest city.

President Muhammadu Buhari

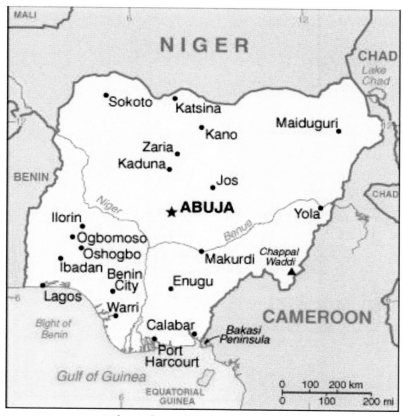

Nigeria - 356,669 sq. mi.

The End

Copyright 2021 Mike Donovan

Made in the USA
Middletown, DE
19 April 2021